Pour mes parents.
R. P.

Couvent Sainte-Cécile, 37 rue Servan, 38000 Grenoble
Loi n° 49 956 du 16 juillet 1949 sur les publications destinées à la jeunesse.

Dépôt légal : février 2022
ISBN : 978-2-344-04991-4 / 001
Achevé d'imprimer en Roumanie en février 2022 par Rotolito Romania.

MIXTE
Issu de sources responsables
FSC® C127233

Richard Petitsigne

Jess Pauwels

Le chevalier Edmond et son cochon

Glénat jeunesse

Dans la salle du trône du château de Chabanais, le vieux seigneur au ventre aussi rebondi qu'une citrouille gourmande discutait avec son chambellan et son fils, le prince Edmond.
C'était un jeune garçon grand et maigre, avec des cheveux roux et le visage moucheté de taches de rousseur.

— Mon fils, commença Fulbert, je vieillis, ainsi devras-tu bientôt prendre ma place sur ce trône.
— On a le temps, répondit d'un ton nonchalant le prince.
— Détrompe-toi, il file très vite. Tu dois maintenant montrer ta valeur ! Il te faut partir en mission dès demain !

Le chambellan Gonfalon remit à Edmond une carte de la terrible contrée voisine : l'empire du Sucre maléfique.

– Vous devrez franchir les obstacles afin de délivrer la princesse retenue prisonnière dans un sombre manoir. Seul un futur chevalier sera capable d'accomplir ces exploits, annonça-t-il.

– Je peux emmener Aristote ? interrogea le prince.

Le vieux seigneur regarda son chambellan, qui leva les yeux au ciel.

– Ton stupide animal ? demanda Fulbert.

– Mon fidèle compagnon ! répliqua Edmond.

– Si tu le dis… Pars avec ta bestiole et ramène-moi cette princesse !

Le lendemain, Edmond chevauchait Aristote, son cochon, et, suivant la carte, s'enfonçait dans la forêt profonde.

— Aristote, mon ami, nous n'allons pas tarder à arriver au lac du Caramel maudit.

— Grouïk, lança le cochon.

— Tu as raison... répondit l'apprenti chevalier.
Edmond ne connaissait pas le langage des cochons, mais il pensa que la réponse de son animal devait vouloir dire : « On va se méfier », ou alors : « Le caramel est mauvais pour les dents ».

Ils arrivèrent devant ce fameux lac et entamèrent la traversée dans le liquide marron, épais et sucré, Edmond cramponné à son cochon.

Ils nageaient depuis un petit moment quand un vent violent se leva.

Bientôt, un tourbillon de caramel mou se forma et entraîna les deux comparses. Grâce à Aristote, qui l'attrapa par le col de son pourpoint, Edmond parvint de l'autre côté du lac, épuisé et tout collant.

L'apprenti chevalier reprit son souffle et tapota le groin de son animal :

— Merci, mon Aristote ! Tu m'as sauvé la vie !

— Groïnk, fit le cochon tout en léchant les vêtements de son maître.

— Ça doit vouloir dire : « De rien », ou : « Je n'ai jamais vu de tourbillon de caramel mou aussi puissant ! », comprit Edmond.

Le duo poursuivit sa route et arriva bientôt face à un nouveau danger : le gouffre de la Méchante Chantilly !
Edmond et son cochon n'eurent pas d'autre choix que de sauter dans le gigantesque trou crémeux.

Pendant la chute, Edmond eut envie de goûter cette chantilly appétissante. Mais, dès qu'il ouvrit la bouche, Aristote la lui ferma de sa patte rose.
Arrivé au fond du gouffre, Edmond découvrit de nombreux squelettes.

— Nom d'un flan à la vanille ! s'exclama-t-il. Cette crème était empoisonnée ?
— Graok ! opina Aristote.
— Ça doit vouloir dire : « Mange de la chantilly et tu finiras tout flapi ».
Que tu es malin, Aristote !

Après un bain dans un ruisseau d'eau, cette fois-ci, pour enlever toute cette mauvaise crème, les deux compères continuèrent leur périple et ne tardèrent pas à tomber sur une autre embûche : le précipice des Sucettes tranchantes !

Ils découvrirent avec horreur un ravin profond d'où surgissait un véritable champ de sucettes pointues et coupantes. Aristote prit son élan et sauta par-dessus la vallée mortelle.
Il atterrit en roulant sur le ventre et fit signe à Edmond d'en faire autant.

L'apprenti chevalier s'élança à son tour, mais il manqua de peu l'autre versant. Heureusement, son cochon le rattrapa et il put rejoindre le sol sain et sauf.

— Merci, mon ami. Décidément, je ne sais pas ce que je ferais sans toi !
— Grouk ! admit Aristote.
— Ça doit vouloir dire : « Tout le plaisir est pour moi », ou : « Il serait temps de reprendre le sport ».

Remis de leurs émotions, les deux amis reprirent leur chemin, qui déboucha au pied d'un manoir lugubre.

— D'après la carte, nous sommes arrivés, mon bon Aristote.

Le jeune homme cogna à la lourde porte et celle-ci s'ouvrit toute seule sur un luxueux salon, richement meublé.
— Entrez, Monsieur, je vous attendais, dit une voix aiguë.

Les deux compères pénétrèrent dans le château et découvrirent une ravissante princesse, assise devant un miroir.
Une servante aux airs doux comme un coulis de framboise était occupée à peigner ses longs cheveux blonds.

— Je suis la princesse Éléonore et voici ma servante Cunégonde. C'est donc vous, le preux chevalier qui doit me sortir de cette sinistre contrée ?

Edmond ne répondit pas. Il semblait subjugué par la suivante.

— Il est vrai, continua la jeune fille, que j'avais espéré un chevalier plus… enfin moins… euh… plus chevalier, quoi !
— Désolé, souffla Edmond.

— Je m'en contenterai, je n'ai guère le choix ! dit la princesse en se pinçant le nez. Mes bagages sont prêts, nous pouvons partir ! Cunégonde, tu es parée ?

— Oui, Madame, chuchota celle-ci.

Aristote remarqua alors qu'Edmond et la servante se miraient en rosissant...

De retour au château, le roi Fulbert de Chabanais retrouva son fils, mais pas de traces d'une princesse à ses côtés.
— Où est la princesse ? s'inquiéta-t-il.
— Finalement, elle est restée au manoir, répondit Edmond. Elle n'a pas supporté que je lui préfère sa servante.

— Tu veux épouser une servante ? lança le souverain, les yeux écarquillés.
— Père, je vous présente Cunégonde, la femme de ma vie, dit le prince en la désignant. Je l'aime et je veux devenir son mari !

— Mais un chevalier ne peut pas prendre une domestique pour épouse ! s'insurgea l'ancien.
— Ça tombe bien, je ne suis pas un chevalier et je ne mérite pas de l'être. Dans cette pièce, seul Aristote est digne de le devenir. Sans lui, je serais mort noyé, empoisonné et déchiqueté. Faites-le chevalier et laissez-moi vivre avec ma bien-aimée !
— Groik ! intervint Aristote.
— Ça doit vouloir dire : « Edmond a raison », ou : « Tout est bon dans ce cochon », conclut Cunégonde.

Quelques semaines plus tard, le royaume fêtait avec faste le mariage d'Edmond et de Cunégonde, sous les regards attendris du vieux seigneur et du premier cochon-chevalier de l'Histoire. Quant à la princesse Éléonore, prise de remords, elle arriva juste à temps et eut un coup de foudre étonnant...

Mini

The story of a Motoring ICON

Contents

Mini

First published in the UK in 2011 by Instinctive Product Development

www.instinctivepd.com

Printed in China

ISBN: 978-1-908816-43-6

Designed by: BrainWave

Creative Director: Kevin Gardner

Written by: Henry Hirst

Images courtesy of Magic Car Pics, Shutterstock, PA Photos and Wiki Commons

Introduction

Voted the second most influential car of the 20th century after the Model T Ford in 1999, the original Mini – as Sir Alec Issigonis' classic design of 1959 inevitably became known – was a car that helped to define an era. Originally perceived in an era when there was the real threat of fuel shortages when Britain and France's disastrous campaign to retake the Suez Canal foundered in international ignominy, no car has perhaps epitomised an era as much as the Mini and the 1960s. In an age when London was swinging, when Carnaby Street and the King's Road in Chelsea were perceived as the style capital of the world, the Mini was the last word in 'cool' motoring. Pictured with the stars of the age, including the designer Mary Quant, the car was to be successful in motor sport and, as one of the last great products of British-designed engineering, it was exported worldwide. It was, perhaps, to reach its ultimate fame in film: if the Volkswagen Beetle was the undoubted star of the film *The Love Bug*, this was nothing to the success of the Minis in *The Italian Job*.

In production for more than 40 years, by which stage almost 5.4 million of the model in its various guises had been made worldwide, the original Mini was to be supplanted in 2000 by a newer and larger model – the MINI – produced, following the takeover of Rover Group (as the manufacturer had become known) by the German company BMW and its partial sale back to a British-owned consortium, at Cowley near Oxford. The new model has proved to be a great success as well with a number of variants and, in 2011, a return to competitive motor rallying. Sales of the new model have been impressive, despite the economic conditions of the past few years, and is now regularly

amongst the top-selling cars in Britain each year.

Although the original Mini was hugely successful, there has been much debate over the years as to how financially profitable it actually was. The reality was that, certainly for the Mark I, the level of profitability was very low and perhaps boosted by the fact that the British Motor Corporation (BMC) accounted for its overheads across the group. The low margins, however, were shown by Ford who examined the new Mini and reckoned that BMC was losing £30 – a considerable sum at the time – on each car sold!

The story of the Mini and MINI in its various guises is enormous and a book such as this can only ever scratch the surface. It is hoped, however, that the content has sufficiently whetted the appetite of the reader for more information. For this reason a selection of further books and other resources with information can be found at the back of the book.

■ **RIGHT: A 1960 colour advert – The Motor.**

■ **BELOW: Maryo Lamothe zips into Turn 1 at the Mont-Tremblant Circuit.**

Development of the Mini

The future Mini was one of a number of new models under development by the BMC in the mid-1950s but the project – designated ADO15 (from the Austin Drawing Office project number) – was prioritised as a result of the Suez Crisis of 1956. In the last great gamble of the British Empire, British and French forces had invaded Egypt following the Nationalisation of the Suez Canal by the Egyptian regime led by Gamal Abd al-Nasser. Worldwide opposition, led by the USA, forced Britain and France into a humiliating retreat and led to a serious supply shortage of oil into the British market. The consequences of this were that demand for fuel-hungry cars collapsed and, for a period, fuel rationing was reintroduced. The scene was set for the development and launch of a radical new small car.

The basic parameters set for the new model were that it should be no longer than 10 feet in length and

■ **ABOVE: The sliding window found on the first Minis.**

■ **LEFT: The transverse engine on the Mark I Mini.**

that the passenger accommodation should occupy 60% of its length. The vehicle was to be a maximum of four feet in height and in width. In order to fulfil these requirements, the new car was designed with its conventional A-series four-cylinder engine mounted transversely with front-wheel drive rather than longitudinally. The vehicle was originally designed with a 948cc engine in mind, although this was replaced by the 848cc model for production. The production version

■ **ABOVE: A new car is born.**

of the car also had the engine rotated 180° in order to reduce icing in the carburettor although this also made the distributor susceptible to water entering through the grille. Although this did save space and has been adopted for most small front-wheel designs subsequently, there were problems in its installation in the Mini, most notably that the air cooling the radiator had already passed over the hot engine and that the ignition system was prone to water entering through the grille. A further space-saving development was the use of compact rubber cones,

■ **ABOVE:** **An advert for the Mini Mark II.**

■ **LEFT:** **A 1959 colour brochure.**

■ **BELOW:** **Now available with two new engines.**

developed by Moulton Developments Ltd, rather than the more usual springs in the suspension.

Other facets of the new car were its sliding windows, which permitted storage in the doors, the monocoque shell, which had welded seams visible on the exterior, and external hinges on the doors and boot. The boot was designed to open outwards in such a way that it could effectively act as a platform in order to increase the luggage space.

Produced from August 1959 through to 1967, the first version of the Mini was the Mark I. Initially marketed under various names, including the Morris Mini-Minor and Austin Seven in the UK, the name Mini was adopted formally in 1961. During its production life, some 1.2 million of the Mark I were constructed. During the eight-year period there were minor updates, including a modified hydrolastic suspension in 1964 and the availability of an automatic version – the Mini-Matic – from 1965. Such was the success

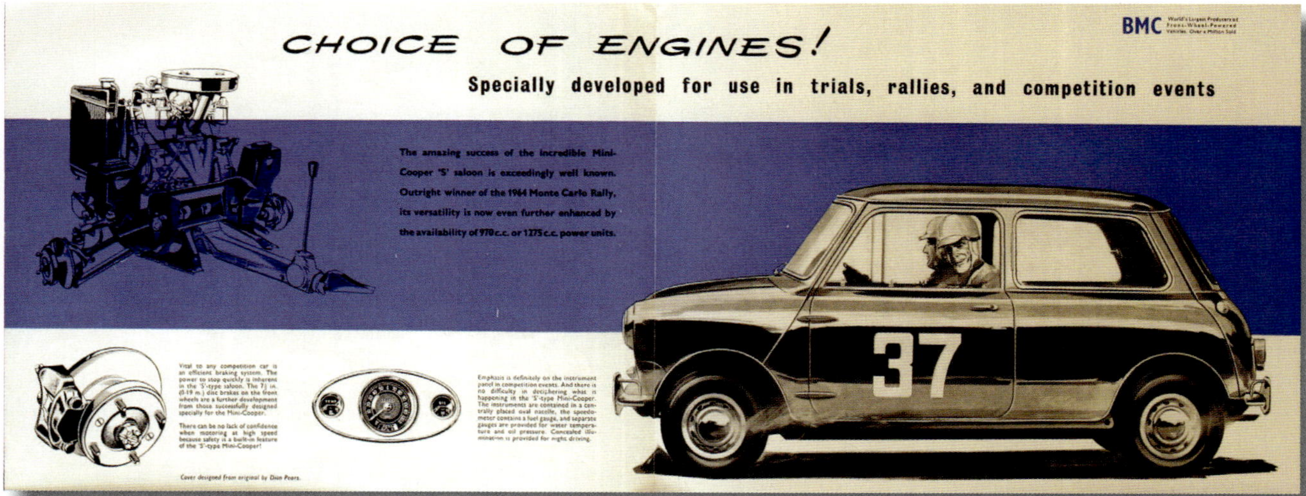

1275 GT
ESTATE
It's too good an

■ **BELOW:** A Mini advert, 1975.

of the Mark I that it was not only manufactured at both Longbridge and Cowley in the UK, but also at factories in Belgium, Chile, Portugal, South Africa and Spain. By the time that production ended, the car was available with three different engine sizes – 850cc, 998cc and 1275cc – and in a considerable variety of body styles.

The next development of the Mini came in 1967 with the launch of the Mark II, which incorporated a redesigned front grille and other modifications. The Mark II was destined to be built for six years and, when production of it ceased in 1973, a total of just over 400,000 had been built. This version was succeeded by the Mark III, which was originally launched in 1969. The new version included a revised body shell, with the external hinges now removed, winding – as opposed to sliding – windows and a return to the cone suspension system rather than the later hydrolastic version. Such were the changes that the factory code was changed to ADO20.

The ADO20 code was also that adopted for the Mini Clubman variant; this version, designed by Roy Haynes, with a modified front end that incorporated sidelights and indicators from the Austin Maxi, had a much squarer appearance. It was produced between 1969 and 1980 primarily at Longbridge but there was also some limited construction undertaken at the factory at Setúbal in Portugal. The model was perceived as a direct replacement for the Riley Elf and Wolseley Hornet versions. A further development saw the launch of the 1275GT; this was a replacement for the Mini Cooper and was produced alongside the Mini Cooper S, which also had a 1275cc engine, until production of the latter ceased in 1971. One significant innovation in 1969 was the use of a printed-circuit board behind the dashboard; the Mini was the first production car to be so fitted. Another innovation, but only as an option (which was generally ignored as a result of the increased noise from the road), was the availability of the Dunlop Denovo tyre for the 1275GT model. These tyres were

■ **ABOVE LEFT AND RIGHT: A Mini 1275GT.**

designed to ensure that the vehicle could continue to operate safely even at high speeds following a puncture. These two models were fitted with the hydrolastic suspension until mid-1971 when the models reverted to the rubber cone suspension that had originally been introduced on the first cars. Production of the Mini Clubman, in both its saloon and estate form, and the Mini 1275GT continued until 1980 by which date almost 500,000 Clubmans and just over 110,000 1275GTs had been constructed.

The models launched in 1969 were destined to be replaced by the Austin Metro, the new small car that was widely perceived to be key to the long-term survival of the manufacturer as a key supplier to the mass British market. Indeed the Metro was branded as the Austin Mini Metro and was soon to outsell its older rival. In 1981 the Mini was the ninth best-selling car in the UK; this was the last time the Mini was to achieve a top-10 finish until the arrival of the MINI some 20 years later. It was perhaps indicative of the future that, in 1981, the Mini Metro was to be the fifth best-selling car in the country. The new car benefited from an automated production line at Longbridge and was itself to become a familiar sight on Britain's roads. Despite the launch of the new model, the traditional Mini continued to be produced in significant numbers.

The launch of the Mini Mark III, also fitted with rubber cone suspension, was to see the end of manufacture of the model at Cowley; thereafter UK production would be limited to Longbridge, although the car was also to be constructed in Spain (Pamplona), Australia (Zetland, New South Wales), Belgium (Seneffe), Portugal (Setúbal), South Africa (Cape Town) and New Zealand (Petone). As the popularity of the model declined, largely as a result of the launch of new and more up-to-date models, production

ceased in many of these overseas factories during the early 1980s.

The Mini Mark III – the branding 'Austin' and 'Morris' was dropped from the car from this version – was to remain in production until 1976 when it was replaced by the Mark IV. As with the Mark III, UK production of the Mark IV was concentrated at Longbridge in the UK with overseas production handled in Spain (Pamplona), Australia (Zetland, New South Wales), Belgium (Seneffe), Portugal (Setúbal), South Africa (Cape Town), Chile (Arica) and New Zealand (Petone). The Mark IV was provided with a revised front-end design that included a rubber-mounted subframe. Internally there were also modifications with the inclusion of larger foot pedals and a twin-stalk indicator. Production of the Mark IV was to continue through to 1984.

In 1984 came the next revision – the Mark V; this and the subsequent Mark VI and Mark VII were only to be manufactured at Longbridge in the UK. The Mark V utilised the same body shell as the Mark IV but was fitted with plastic wheel arches and 210mm brake discs. The Mark V was the last version of the car to be produced with the 998cc engine; in later years only a 1275cc version was available. The Mark VI was introduced in 1990 and the Mark VII in 1996; the body style of these last two versions was largely unchanged with the major modifications taking place internally. For example, the Mark VII included an airbag in order to ensure that it fulfilled European legislation.

Although the main model was not to see significant change during these last years, the popularity of the model increased as a result of the large number of limited edition and retro cars

■ LEFT: Former Prime Minister Gordon Brown during the official opening of BMW's new MINI car plant at Cowley, near Oxford.

■ BELOW: An Austin Metro.

that were produced; details of many of these can be found in the final chapter of this book covering customisation and variants. However, the writing was on the wall for the 40-year-old Mini; following the sale of much of the business to the Phoenix consortium, BMW retained the rights to the Mini name and licensed the new company to continue production of the traditional model for a period. The final 'traditional' Mini – a red Cooper S – was built at Longbridge in October 2000. This car is now preserved at the British Motor Industry Heritage Trust at Gaydon in Warwickshire; the car is also commemorated by a limited edition 1:36 diecast model produced by Corgi.

Development of the new MINI commenced in 1995 and was launched formally in 2001. With a design team led by Frank Stephenson, the model was inspired by the original Issigonis design but the new car is

■ **TOP: End of production; the final classic edition of the Mini Cooper.**

■ **ABOVE: A BMW MINI Cooper.**

significantly longer (at, originally, 142.8 inches), wider (at 66.5 inches) and taller (at, originally, 55.9 inches), than its predecessor. Although production of the original Mark I model was planned for Longbridge, the dismemberment of the erstwhile Rover Group by BMW saw Cowley become the designated manufacturing plant. The car was powered by one of three different Tritec petrol engines, rated at between 1.4 and 1.6 litres depending upon the model supplied and one Toyota 1.4 litre engine for the diesel market. Although the majority of Mark Is supplied were standard units, a MINI Cooper and a MINI Cooper S – the latter being fitted with a supercharged 1.6 litre engine – were also available. For certain markets, such as the USA and Australia where air conditioning was considered essential, only the Cooper and Cooper S models were supplied as it was believed that the basic engine lacked the power to support the air conditioning. Initially production was solely hardtop; however, in 2005 a convertible version of the Mark I was launched.

Production of the Mark 1 hardtop continued until 2006 and that of the convertible until 2008; in November 2006 came the launch of the new MINI

■ **RIGHT: A 2009 BMW MINI Cooper S.**

■ **BELOW: A MINI Mark 1 Convertible.**

Mark II. Although clearly derived from the earlier model, the Mark II has a number of significant changes. The overall length of the car has been increased by just over two inches as a result of new safety requirements, the arrangement and location of the sidelights and headlights have been altered and the grille has been modified. In order to accommodate these changes, virtually every body panel has been subtly altered. In addition, the car now came with a new range of engines, the Prince 1.4 litre (in the Mark II MINI One), the Prince 1.6 litre (in the MINI Cooper), the 1.6 litre Peugeot diesel engine (for diesel versions of the One and Cooper) and the 1.6 litre turbocharged Prince (for the MINI Cooper S); the majority of these engines are now manufactured at BMW's engine works at Hams Hall near Birmingham. The model range started with the hardtop and with a Clubman, effectively an estate version of the car, in 2007; this was added to by a convertible version in 2009. In terms of body style, there are four versions: a three-door hatchback; a five-door estate; a two-door convertible; and a five-door crossover SUV.

Alec Issigonis: Master of Design

Although by the time he died in October 1988 at the age of 81, Alec Issigonis had been knighted and become a Fellow of the Royal Society, his background was not one that marked him out as one of the saviours of the British motor industry.

Alexander Arnold Constantine Issigonis was, in fact, born in Smyrna in 1906 as the son of a Greek father and a mother of German ancestry. His father's family had originally emigrated to this region of the Ottoman Empire in the 1830s. His grandfather worked for the British-built Smyrna-Aydin Railway and thus acquired British nationality, which was passed down through successive generations. This factor was to be of great importance when in 1922, after the Greco-Turkish War that had started in 1919, much of the city was destroyed by fire and was re-occupied by the Turks. As British subjects, the Issigonis family was amongst those evacuated by the Royal Marines and, following a stay in Malta (where his father died), Issigonis and his mother arrived in Britain in 1923, where he completed his education.

His career in the motor industry started when he joined Humber as an engineer and designer; however, it was

■ **TOP INSET: A 1955 Humber Super Snipe.**

■ **RIGHT: A 1975 Maxi advert.**

■ TOP INSET: **A 1964 Austin 1800.**

■ ABOVE: **Morris Minors at Chatsworth House.**

■ BELOW: **Sir Alec Issigonis.**

his early success in motor sport, where he drove a modified Austin Seven, that led him to join the Austin company. In 1936, he moved to Austin's great competitor, Morris at Cowley, where he was to remain until 1955. During this period he was to design another classic of the British motor industry – the Morris Minor – that was to remain in production from 1948 through to 1971.

Back with Austin (by now known as the BMC), Issigonis was tasked with the development of a range of new motorcars for his new employer. However, following the Suez Crisis and the imposition of fuel rationing, he was told to concentrate upon the smallest of the three models – codenamed XC/9003 – which was to be launched in August 1959 as the Morris Mini Minor and the Austin Seven – although, inevitably, it soon became known as the Mini.

Following the successful development of the Mini, Issigonis became Technical Director of the BMC in 1961 and was to be involved in the development of many of the most notable products of the company from this period. His designs included the Morris 1100, the Austin 1800 and the Austin Maxi. He became a Fellow of the Royal Society in 1967 and was knighted two years later; however, also in 1969, with the creation of British Leyland, his influence waned and he officially retired in 1971 although he remained active in the industry until his death.

John Cooper

COOPER S · CONVERSIONS · ACCESSORIES · PERSONAL ACCESSORIES

The Mini and Motor Sport

■ BELOW: A 1963 Mini Cooper S.

■ BOTTOM: A 1973 Innocenti Mini Cooper S.

Although Issigonis was originally reluctant to see the Mini adapted for use in motor sport, his friend John Cooper of the Cooper Car Company had other ideas. Despite the designer's reluctance, Cooper, who had had experience in Formula One and car rallying, went over his friend's head and got an agreement for the development of a performance car from the BMC board.

With approval for the project given, Issigonis and Cooper co-operated on the development of the first Mini Cooper. The Austin Mini Cooper and the Morris Mini Cooper were both launched in 1961. The car was fitted with an upgraded version of the original 848cc engine that was provided with a longer stroke in order to increase capacity to 997cc (replaced by a shorter stroke 998cc engine in 1964). This resulted in an increase in the engine's power from 34 to 55bhp. Also fitted were front disc brakes, a closer ratio gearbox and twin SU carburettors. In order to satisfy the regulations for entry into Group 2 rally racing, a total of 1,000 of the model were ordered. Two years later a more powerful version of the Mini Cooper – the Mini Cooper S – was launched. This included a larger (1071cc) engine as well as other modifications. A total of 4,030 Mini Cooper S models were completed before the car was updated in August 1964. Two other versions of the Cooper S – with either a 970cc or a 1275cc engine – were also produced with production of only 963 of the former

Mini Cooper S hustles to an outright win in the Monte Carlo Rally

(Photograph reproduced by permission of "Motor Sport")

BMC leads in other things too

BMC, as you may have heard, won the Monte. And added one more achievement to a list as long as your arm. But BMC leadership is not confined to the rally circuit.

Take Choice

BMC makes 39 different cars. More than any other manufacturer in Europe. Why so many? Because BMC believes that cars should be as individual as people. And a wide range means that a motorist can choose the car that fits his needs like a glove.

Take Design

Follow-my-leader design is out at BMC. Here design is original and lasting, built on forward-thinking and not a sudden whim. So you won't find BMC cars here today and gone tomorrow, slaves to fashion and overnight depreciation. At BMC, cars are designed *around people* . . . with plenty of leg, head, luggage and elbow-room.

Take Engineering

Engineering goes hand-in-hand with design at BMC. Hence the transverse engine of the Minis and 1100 series . . . developed to allow more passenger-space to be designed into a car. BMC has the lead in suspension too: Hydrolastic® gives the sort of ride you get in cars costing very much more.

Five years ago, not one front-wheel-drive vehicle was made by a British manufacturer. Today BMC is the world's largest producer of front-wheel-drive vehicles—and already over a million have been made. BMC leadership . . . again!

AUSTIN · AUSTIN-HEALEY · MORRIS · MG · RILEY · WOLSELEY · VANDEN PLAS PRINCESS

THE BRITISH MOTOR CORPORATION LTD

BIRMINGHAM AND OXFORD

C

before production ceased in 1965. In all, production of Mini Coopers in Britain before production ceased in 1971 – allegedly due to an unwillingness on the part of British Leyland to pay royalties to John Cooper for his design – totalled some 83,000 Mark Is (split between 64,000 for the basic Mini Cooper and 19,000 Cooper Ss), just over 22,000 Mark IIs (of which 16,000 were Coopers and 6,300 were Cooper Ss) and 1,570 Mark IIIs (all of which were Cooper Ss). Although UK production of the Mini Cooper ceased in 1971, the design was licensed to the Italian company Innocenti in 1971 and two years later to the Spanish manufacturer Automoviles de Turismo Hispano-Ingleses (Authi).

Part of the rationale for the development of the Mini Cooper

■ **LEFT: The 1966 Monte Carlo winners, Timo Mäkinen and Paul Easter, in action.**

■ **ABOVE: The 1964 Monte Carlo winners, Paddy Hopkirk and Henry Liddon, receive their trophy from Princess Grace of Monaco and Prince Rainier III.**

was to facilitate the marque's entry into motor sport and, during the 1960s, the Mini was to achieve some considerable success in the Monte Carlo Rally. In 1962 the Ladies' Prize was won by Pat Moss and her co-driver Ann Wisdom. In three years – 1964, 1965 and 1967 – the Mini won the rally with cars driven by Paddy Hopkirk and co-driver Henry Liddon, Timo Mäkinen with Paul Easter, and Rauno Aaltonen with Henry Liddon, respectively. In 1966 three Minis, led by Timo Mäkinen with Paul Easter finished in the top three places. The cars were all disqualified as a result of a technicality over the use of a variable-resistance dimming

■ **ABOVE: Rauno Aaltonen, left, and Henry Liddon of Finland are in their BMC Cooper after being placed third in the Monte Carlo Rally which finished in Monaco.**

circuit in the headlamps rather than the prescribed dual-filament circuit. Curiously, following the decision by the French judges to disqualify the British-built cars, the winner was a French-built Citroën driven by Pauli Toivonen.

Following the 1968 Monte Carlo Rally, when the Minis finished third, fourth and fifth, Mini ceased to be entered for that competition.

It wasn't only in the Monte Carlo Rally that the Mini Cooper had success; the car was to win the European Rally Championship on two occasions: in 1965 when the title was won by the Finn Rauno Aaltonen and the following year when the G2 section was won by the Pole Sobieslaw Zasada. In 1963 the Swede Bengt Söderström won the 14th International Swedish Rally, the only occasion that the race was won by a Mini. Rauno Aaltonen was also to win, with co-driver Bob Holden, the Gallaher 500 at Mount Panorama, Bathurst, in New South Wales, Australia in 1966. Although this was the only time that the race was won by a Mini, Paddy

AUTOCAR, 3 December 1965

23

BMC WINS RAC RALLY FOR BRITAIN!

Outright win for Mini Cooper S – also 1st in Touring Category. Austin-Healey 3000 2nd overall and 1st in GT Category. 14th outright international rally win this year for BMC – Europe's top rally team!

RAC RALLY : BMC SCORECARD

OUTRIGHT WINNER
MINI COOPER S
Rauno Aaltonen/Tony Ambrose

2nd OVERALL
AUSTIN-HEALEY 3000
Timo Makinen/Paul Easter

Class 3 Touring Category (850cc – 1000cc)
MINI COOPER S
1st Ron Maple/George Marrs

Class 4 Touring Category (1001cc – 1300cc)
MINI COOPER S
1st Rauno Aaltonen/Tony Ambrose
2nd Lars Ytterbring/R. Hakansson
3rd Tony Fall/Ron Crellin

Class 10 GT Category (1001cc – 1300cc)
MINI COOPER S
1st Jorma Lusenius/Mike Wood
2nd Paddy Hopkirk/Henry Liddon

Classes 12/13 (comb.) GT Category (over 1600cc)
AUSTIN-HEALEY 3000
1st Timo Makinen/Paul Easter

LOMBANK ECURIE TEAM PRIZE
MINI COOPER S
J. Bloxham/V. Bond
AUSTIN MINI
G. R. Hudson-Evans/J. Spencer
AUSTIN MINI
A. Fisher/B. Harper

Subject to official confirmation

THE BRITISH MOTOR CORPORATION LTD
LONGBRIDGE, BIRMINGHAM

F

■ **ABOVE: Rauno Aaltonen with his BMC Cooper 5.**

Hopkirk also raced at the circuit on three occasions between 1965 and 1967; his best result was in 1965 when he finished third in his class and sixth overall. In 1965 Rauno Aaltonen partnered by the British driver Tony Ambrose won the 14th RAC Rally in Britain; this was the only occasion that this rally was won by a Mini, the car in question being a Mini Cooper S 1275. Also in 1965 the Finnish pairing of Timo Mäkinen and Pekka Keskitalo won the Finnish 1000 Lakes Rally. In 1966 the Scottish Rally was won by Tony Fall and Mike Wood in a Mini Cooper S.

Almost from the start of the Mini's career it had been involved in motor sport, although initially this was unofficial. Although the early Minis lacked speed, they more than made up for this with their manoeuvrability and cornering. The marque's first success in the prestigious British Saloon (now Touring) Car Championships came

BMC WINS IN TULIP RALLY!

- BEST PERFORMANCE OVERALL – MINI COOPER 'S' (1300)
- OUTRIGHT WIN G.T. CATEGORY – AUSTIN-HEALEY 3000 Mk III
- OUTRIGHT WIN TOURING CATEGORY – MINI COOPER 'S' (1300)
- MANUFACTURER'S TEAM PRIZE – MINI COOPER 'S'
- 3 CLASS WINS

BMC HAS NOW WON ALL THREE MAJOR EUROPEAN RALLIES THIS YEAR

A Mini Cooper 'S' won the 1964 Monte Carlo Rally, and also landed outright victory in this year's Circuit of Ireland Rally.

Like all the big European rallies, the Tulip is a brutal test of driving skill and engineering expertise. The route this year took in France, Belgium, Holland, Luxembourg and Germany, with short, sharp skirmishes round the famous Nurburgring and Zandvoort race-circuits—and several tough hill climbs. Altogether 1750 miles were covered, through breathtaking country at heartstopping speeds.

The Austin Healey 3000 on its way to an outright win in the G.T. Category.

Apart from tuning and very-necessary rally equipment, the BMC cars entered in the Tulip Rally were exactly the same as the cars you can buy in your local showroom ...right down to the floor-mats!
The fantastic success of BMC cars in the Tulip Rally highlights the strength, performance, roadholding and dependability that BMC builds into every production car. Features that are just as welcome on an international rally as they are on a trip to the coast.

BMC TULIP RALLY SUCCESSES

Best Performance and outright winner Touring Category
MINI COOPER 'S' (1300)
Timo Makinen & Tony Ambrose

Outright winner G.T. Category
AUSTIN-HEALEY 3000 MK III
Donald & Erle Morley

Manufacturer's Team Prize
MINI COOPER 'S'

G.T. cars over 2500 cc
1st & 3rd – AUSTIN-HEALEY 3000

G.T. cars 1000-1300 cc
1st & 2nd – MINI COOPER 'S'

Touring Cars 1000-1300 cc
FIRST SIX PLACES – MINI COOPER 'S'

Results subject to official confirmation

THE BRITISH MOTOR CORPORATION LTD
BIRMINGHAM AND OXFORD

in 1961 when Sir John Whitmore not only won his class but also came out as overall champion in his works' Mini. This was to be the first of a number of overall triumphs during the decade. The following year the title was won by John Love driving a Mini Cooper for Vita Racing. In 1963 Sir John Whitmore was to come second in his works' Cooper. The following year another Mini Cooper was to come second, this time driven by John Fitzpatrick. The Mini was to triumph once more during the 1960s, when in 1969, Alec Poole won in his Mini Cooper S on behalf of the Equipe Arden team. In the late 1970s there were to be two further wins when, in 1978 and 1979, Richard Longman won with his privately-entered Mini 1275GT.

But the Mini Cooper would make a comeback to the company's product range after a gap of 20 years in 1990. The popularity of the Rover Special Products (RSP) in 1990 led to a new

■ **ABOVE: Paddy Hopkirk fends off late-breaking team-mate John Fitzpatrick.**
■ **BELOW: A car in the 2006 MINI Challenge.**

■ **ABOVE: A MINI John Cooper Works GP.**

Mini Cooper being launched; this entered full production in 1992. This model was fitted with a multi-point fuel-injected 1275cc engine. By the time production of the original Mini ceased in 2000, the Mini Classic Cooper and the Mini Classic Cooper S were amongst the four versions still produced.

Whilst the original Mini faded from motor sport, BMW as the successors to the rights to the Mini name have continued to develop the brand as a performance car. From the start of production of the new MINI a Cooper and a Cooper S version were both available, both of which were fitted with the 1.6 litre Tritec I4 engine with that supplied for the Cooper S being supercharged. In 2006 a limited production run of 2,000 of the MINI John Cooper Works GP were manufactured. Available in only one colour scheme – thunder blue with silver roof – each car was individually numbered. This was the last Mark I variant of the new MINI to be built using the Tritec engine.

The launch of the Mark II in 2006 also saw Cooper and Cooper S versions, this time with both cars fitted with the Prince 1.6 litre engine with that fitted to the Cooper S being supercharged. As with the Mark I version, there have been a number of special edition cars that emphasise the model's performance. The MINI John Cooper Works Challenge, unveiled at the IAA Motor Show in 2007, was based on the R56 Hardtop – all MINI models have an R-series code-number, a reflection of the model's original development by the Rover Group – and built by BMW's motor sport factory in Munich, where the company also handles work on Formula One racing cars and vehicles aimed at the European touring competition. Launched at the Geneva Motor Show in 2008 and available from 2009, the MINI John Cooper Works comes in three variants: the Hardtop; the Clubman; and, the Convertible. Based around the MINI Mark II Cooper S, the model is fitted with a higher-output engine and a six-speed Getrag manual gearbox along with numerous other modifications. All come badged as 'John Cooper Works' rather than the more usual Cooper S.

Launched at the 2009 Mini United Festival at Silverstone to mark the 50th anniversary of the Formula One championship won by Jack Brabham in a Cooper-designed and built car, the MINI John Cooper works World Championship 50 is a limited edition of 250 – later increased to 500 – cars.

It's not just in the retention and the development of the MINI Cooper that the new model plays homage to the heritage of its illustrious antecedents. Since 2004 it has been possible to race the MINI in the annual MINI Challenge. For 2011, the competition includes stages in Argentina, Brazil, Germany and Spain. The competition is open to all drivers aged 18 and over who are in possession of a National A or International B/C competition licence. All drivers operate with identical vehicles – the MINI John Cooper Works Challenge. In addition to this competition, it has also been announced that MINI is resuming its love affair with rallying for the 2011 season and will line up at selected events in the FIA World Rally Championship (WRC).

The Swinging Sixties

If ever a car can be said to have epitomised an era, it was the Mini and the 1960s. The mood was one of great change and, for a period, it seemed as though Britain and British design were again at the centre of the world's attention.

The Swinging Sixties represented years when anything seemed to be possible; Britain was becoming much more tolerant as a society as attitudes

■ **LEFT: After being banned for over 30 years, D H Lawrence's book, *Lady Chatterley's Lover*, sells out hours after being released.**

■ **BELOW: Three original 1960s Mini Coopers, used by Paramount Pictures to promote the 1969 film *The Italian Job*.**

■ **ABOVE: A scene from the controversial 'hippie' musical *Hair*.**

changed and as some of the more restrictive aspects of life from earlier years disappeared or were under severe threat.

The decade started with the prosecution for obscenity of Penguin Books for the publication of D. H. Lawrence's explicit final novel *Lady Chatterley's Lover*. Following the trial, in which the publisher was acquitted, a second edition of the book was published which included the dedication: 'For having published this book, Penguin Books were prosecuted under the Obscene Publications Act, 1959 at the Old Bailey in London from 20 October to 2 November 1960. This edition is therefore dedicated to the twelve jurors, three women and nine men, who returned a verdict of "Not Guilty" and thus made D. H. Lawrence's last novel available for the first time to the public in the United Kingdom.'

Penguin had been prosecuted under the 1959 Obscenity Act that

ABOVE INSET: **Twiggy.**

allowed for the defence of artistic merit. Another area of the arts that was to be considerably liberalised was the theatre. Up until 1968, when the role was abolished as a result of the Theatres Act, the Lord Chamberlain had the function of granting a licence to all plays put on the stage in London and was, thus, effectively the censor of British drama. The London opening of the stage musical *Hair: The American Tribal Love-Rock Musical* with its prominent stage nudity was delayed until 1969 and the passing of the act.

If the arts were becoming more permissive, so too was personal morality. Although homosexuality was illegal until 1967 when consensual sex between those aged 21 and over was legalised, this reform had been foreshadowed by the Wolfenden

■ ABOVE INSET: **The Beatles perform on the CBS *Ed Sullivan Show* in New York, in 1964.**

■ ABOVE: **A MINI driving up to the Abbey Road crossing made famous by the Beatles.**

Report of 1957. Oral contraception began to be widely available from the early years of the decade and, following David Steel's pioneering Abortion Bill of 1967, back-street abortionists became increasingly a thing of the past.

The permissive society had been born and, with it, London seemed to become the style capital of the world. In its issue of 15 April 1966 magazine caught the spirit of the age when it referred to 'swinging London' and the name also caught on with one of the numerous pirate radio stations of the era – Swinging Radio England. In fashion, influential designers such as Mary Quant came to the fore

- **ABOVE RIGHT: The Earl of Snowdon is pictured leaving Clarence House, London in a white Mini.**
- **RIGHT: Peter Sellers drives a Circassian blue Mini – a birthday present to his wife, Britt Ekland – through a gigantic cake after officially opening the new showroom for Harold Radford, Hammersmith, London.**
- **BELOW: Spike Milligan.**

whilst British models, such as Jean Shrimpton and Twiggy, were perhaps to become the world's first supermodels.

In music – with groups such as the Beatles, the Kinks, the Rolling Stones and the Who – British music was at the forefront of the latest developments of popular music, leading the so-called 'British invasion' of the all-important American market whilst other British groups, such as Cream and Pink Floyd, were also key to the development of psychedelic rock. In cinema, British film was also influential with classics such as *Alfie* (1966), *Blow-up* (1966), *Georgy Girl* (1966) and *If...* (1968).

Gradually one symbol came to evoke the spirit of the 1960s – the Union Flag – and when the first classic Mini, owned by the actor Noel Harrison, painted as though the Union Jack flag had been draped over the car appeared, the Mini itself became inextricably linked with the Swinging Sixties. A second Mini painted the same way appeared at the British pavilion at the World's Fair in Montreal in 1967. The red, white and blue of the Union Flag was emphasised in perhaps the greatest of all car movies *The Italian Job* in which three Mini Cooper S cars appear in a dramatic car chase in the streets of Turin.

The counter-culture seal of approval for the Mini was emphasised by the number of celebrities of the period that bought either the standard car or had bespoke versions created for them. The noted comic actor Peter Sellers was one notable purchaser whilst other celebrity owners of the Mini included his then wife Britt Ekland, who drove a Mini de Ville designed by Radford. Other Mini de Ville owners included Ringo Starr, John Lennon and Marianne Faithfull, who famously appeared with her two-tone car outside the Law Courts in London to hear the results of Mick Jagger's appeal against his conviction for drug use in 1967. The other members of the Beatles – Paul McCartney with a Radford Cooper S, John Lennon with his black Radford Cooper S with its blacked-out windows, black bumpers and black wheels, and George Harrison with his psychedelic Cooper (that once featured as a Cargo diecast model) – also owned Minis. Another famous musician to own a Mini was Michael Nesmith of The Monkees, who owned a customised Mini Cooper S. Apart from Peter Sellers, another Goon – Spike Milligan – was also an enthusiastic owner of a Mini. Beyond the worlds of music and comedy, the Mini was also owned by a host of the rich and famous from the period, including the Royal Family when Lord Snowdon acquired one as did the late King Hussein of Jordan. Other noted actors to have owned Minis include Clint Eastwood, James Garner, Tom Hanks, Steve McQueen, David Niven and Mickey Rourke whilst owners from the world of fashion have included Twiggy and Kate Moss.

RADFORD
RADFORD

Worth looking at . . .
The new Austin Seven is a car worth looking at. On both the B.M.C.'s new babies (the Austin Seven and the Mini-Minor) you may specify SMITHS heating and demisting equipment, and SMITHS Radiomobile car radio, as optional extras. The SMITHS instruments on the dashboard match the car in efficiency and design, and the accurate information they provide contributes equally to safe driving and to proper maintenance. They are worth looking at, too.
SMITHS
a name with a world of meaning
YON 956
SMITHS INSTRUMENTS
SMITHS CAR HEATERS
SMITHS RADIOMOBILE
K.L.G. SPARKING PLUGS
BLUECOL ANTI-FREEZE
PETROFLEX TUBING
SMITHS BATTERIES
SMITHS
MOTOR ACCESSORY DIVISION • CRICKLEWOOD WORKS, LONDON N.W.2

Everyday Life

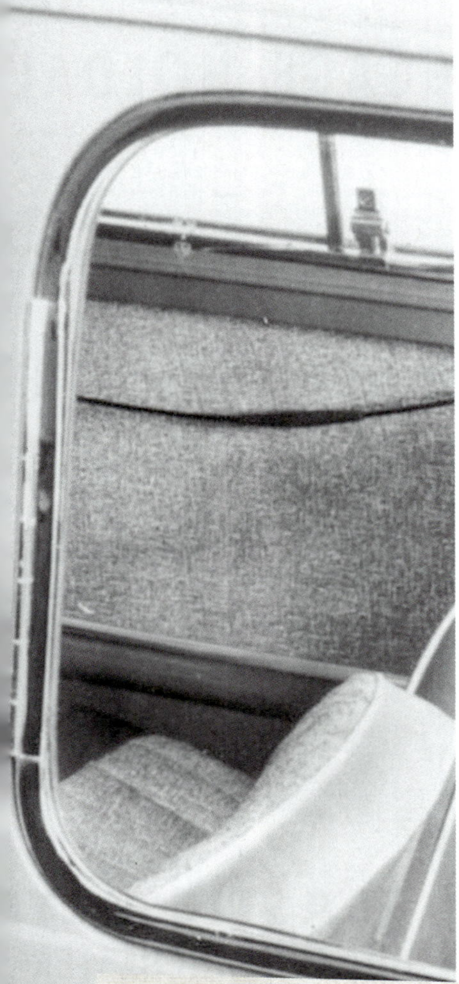

When the Mini was launched in 1959, the UK car manufacturing industry dominated its home market and, through subsidiaries overseas, British-designed cars were manufactured in many other parts of the world. Few British drivers would have dreamt of buying a car that had been produced outside the country and there was a thriving export trade to those countries where the British Motor Corporation didn't have its own works. The original Mark I Mini was, moreover, produced in Australia, Belgium and Portugal as well as both Cowley and Longbridge in the United Kingdom. Fast forward 50 years and, such has been the change in the market that some 80% of new UK car purchases are of models manufactured abroad – although, as with Ford, these may have a significant UK content such is the nature of the global car trade – and up to 80% of production of the new MINI is now exported.

When first launched in 1959, the standard Mini cost £350 excluding the Purchase Tax of almost £147. This car came without a heater or radio; these cost purchasers an additional £6.50 and £18.00 respectively. A deluxe version of the car was also available; this cost an additional £28.50 over and above the cost of the standard model as well as a further £13.00 in Purchase Tax. For this expenditure, the purchaser got a car that included the heater as well as better internal upholstery and colour co-ordinated carpet. Today the model range starts at just under £12,000. Whilst there would appear to have been a dramatic increase in price, in real terms the cost of the car has diminished if compared with average house prices (after all, for most people, the car represents the second most expensive item after the house ever acquired). In 1959 the price of the average house sold in the United Kingdom for £2,500; in other words, the price of the Mini (excluding tax) represented 14% of the price of the average house. In 2009, the price of the average house was £162,000 thus making the price of the new MINI only 7.5% of the cost.

What did the purchaser of the new Mini get in 1959? Without a heater and radio, the standard model was basic; it was effectively two small boxes – the passenger and engine compartments – on four wheels. Storage was limited behind the rear passenger seats – hence the design of the hinged boot door to increase capacity – and there was also storage in the side compartments inserted within each of the side doors (with dimensions large enough, it was alleged, to accommodate a gin bottle). The car was undoubtedly small and fuel efficient, having no serious domestic rival for size until the launch of the Hillman Imp in 1963, but generally speaking cars of the era were smaller than those produced in

the 21st century. Safety regulations and other legal requirements have made modern cars much more complex and the population itself has, as a result of improved diet and growing levels of obesity, grown larger as well.

When the car was first launched, the magazine *The Motor* undertook a test of one of the deluxe models. The magazine found that the car had a top speed just in excess of 70mph, could accelerate from 0 to 60mph in just over 27 seconds and had a fuel consumption of 43.5mpg.

One of the criticisms of the modern MINI is that it is much larger and more highly engineered than the original. Alex Moulton, who designed the suspension for the original Mini, commented to *MiniWorld* in April 2006 'It's enormous – the original Mini was the best packaged car of all time – this is an example of how not to do it. It's huge on the outside and weighs the same as an Austin Maxi. The crash protection has been taken too far. I mean, what do you want, an armoured car?' Safety is an issue with any car; modern requirements – such as airbags – have undoubtedly led to major improvements in safety although Issigonis was always a firm believer in safety and the original Mini was designed to be as safe as possible.

Whilst Issigonis was undoubtedly keen to promote the safety aspects of the Mini, other aspects of the design did, undoubtedly, cause problems. Mention has already been made to the fact that the production models of the original Mini had the engine rotated 180° to reduce icing and the fact that this led to the distributor being susceptible to water ingress through the grille. This was not the only quirk of design that affected everyday use of the car. Early production models suffered from water getting into the passenger compartment and this led to dampness and ultimately an unpleasant odour; one of the factors behind this was the summer of 1959 – when the car was being tested – was particularly dry and hot, with the result that serious water penetration wasn't discovered until the weather deteriorated later in the year. Another problem was that, for those cars fitted with an internal heater, this was not good enough to prevent from misting up during cold weather – a problem, it has to be noted, that afflicts most British-built cars of a certain age. There were also problems with balancing the brakes of the front-wheel car, the clutch and with noise from the fan. As with all new cars, however, these faults were gradually identified and addressed.

DECEMBER 30, 1959
The Motor
EVERY WEDNESDAY
ONE SHILLING
XXA 354
NEW BREED OF SMALL CAR!
AUSTIN
se7en
Small size outside (ten feet long). Big size inside (four grown-ups). Full-size engine (4 cylinder, 848 cc). Right-size price (under £500) and up to 50 mpg, over 70 mph.
BMC
AUSTIN
LOOKS
YEARS
AHEAD
THE AUSTIN MOTOR COMPANY LIMITED · LONGBRIDGE · BIRMINGHAM

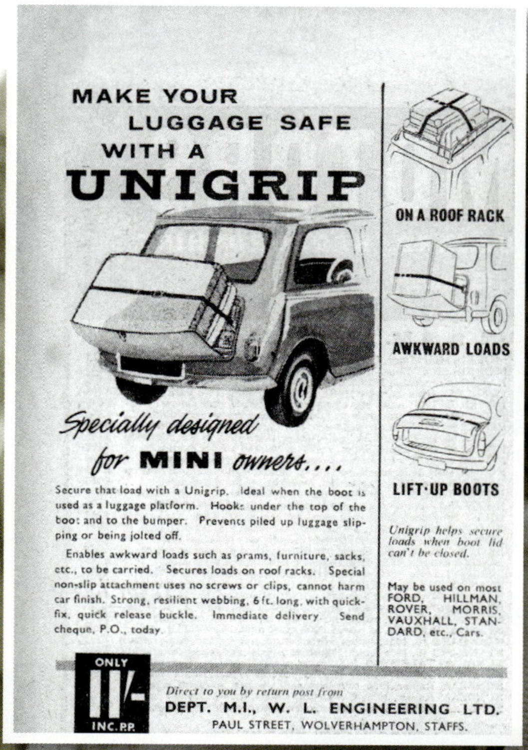

■ **RIGHT:** A publicity shot of Alec Issigonis, the designer of the Mini.

The BEST DRESSED
'BABIES'
WEAR
COSMIC
ACCESSORIES
REAR WHEEL SPATS
(in Austin and Mini Colours)
These beautifully styled pressings give the Mini and Austin 7 a low sleek distinctive look, whilst being functional in keeping mud and spray down to a minimum. Simple to fit or remove.
Price £4.10.0. Pair. Carr. Paid
INTERIOR DOOR HANDLES
Die cast, polished alloy handles improve the interior finish and offer less opportunity for children to inadvertently open the doors. Simple and quick to fit.
Price £1. 0. 0. Pair. Carriage Paid
COMBINED GRILLE, STONE, SPLASH GUARD
This attractive aluminium grille especially enhances the Mini Minor. The grille surround is rolled aluminium channel and the centre embellishing strip is stainless steel, neither of which can rust. Fitted quickly and simply with four chrome plated knurled nuts and die cast clamps.
Price £2. 19. 6. Carriage Paid
CENTRE BONNET, EMBELLISHING STRIP
This heavily chrome plated brass strip runs the length of the bonnet and fits neatly over the existing raised beading. Sliding bolts and nuts supplied.
Price 15s. 0d. Carriage Paid
MINI & AUSTIN 7 DOOR SILL KICKING STRIPS 30/- per pair
Literature sent free on request to Dept. M.3.
COSMIC CAR ACCESSORIES LTD.
BESCOT STREET · WALSALL
Telephone: WALSALL 27188/9

The Germans Arrive

By the early 1970s, as a result of mergers and acquisitions, the British Leyland Motor Corporation (BLMC) had grown to become one of the biggest motor manufacturers in the world, with massive production of cars, commercial vehicles and buses both in the UK and around the world. But not all was well with the business, however, as poor labour relations, an inadequate product range, the threat of imported vehicles – in particular those from Japan – and a reputation for a lack of quality in the finished product all combined to bring the business to its knees.

In 1975, with the business all but bankrupt, BLMC was effectively nationalised and a restructuring and retrenchment policy was introduced. The number of factories that the car business employed was reduced and the product range streamlined and modernised with some success; the Mini, however, continued to be produced in significant numbers throughout this period. During its period of public ownership, the business was to change with subsidiaries, such as Jaguar, privatised prior to the company changing its name to Rover Group in 1986. In 1987 the truck business was merged with the Dutch business DAF and the following year there was a management buy-out of the bus and coach division. The rump of Rover Group – effectively the mass car business with its factories at Longbridge and Cowley – was

■ **TOP: Longbridge.**

■ **ABOVE: The 5,000,000th car comes off the production line at British Leyland.**

sold to British Aerospace in 1988 but this ownership was destined to be short-lived and the company was again sold, this time to the German car manufacturer BMW in 1994. It was whilst under BMW ownership that the decision to cease production of the traditional Mini was taken.

Development work on the replacement MINI – the new model has its name capitalised to distinguish it from the 'classic' model – started in 1995 at Rover's site at Gaydon in Warwickshire and in Germany. The British designers initially favoured a more economic version with the Germans backing a sportier model; ultimately, it was the German concept that won through. During this period, however, the future of the Rover Group operations again came under question with BMW ultimately deciding to divest itself of the Longbridge operation but retain the Cowley factory in Oxford for production of the new model.

The sale of the Longbridge site and the remaining parts of the old Rover Group was originally to be made in to a venture capital business but the outcry over the resulting possible job losses led to a new consortium – Phoenix Venture Holdings – offering to acquire the whole Longbridge operation. The consortium, formed by four local businessmen, proved successful and the business, now known as MG Rover, was to lead briefly to a revival of a British-owned mass car manufacturer. The success, however, was not to last long as the business collapsed in April 2005 during the General Election campaign of that year. The remains of the business were acquired by a Chinese car manufacturer and, although limited MG production resumed at Longbridge in 2009, the bulk of the once massive Austin factory has been cleared for redevelopment.

Whilst the story at Longbridge is one of disaster, the reverse is true at Cowley where the new MINI goes from strength to strength.

■ TOP: The production line for the new MINI at the BMW plant in Cowley, Oxford.

The Mini in Popular Culture

Widely regarded as one of the greatest British films of all time, *The Italian Job* of 1969 saw three Mark II Minis, painted (patriotically) red, white and blue, involved in a gold heist in Turin. Directed by Peter Collinson and starring Michael Caine, the film was notable for the chase sequence in which the Minis, driven by members of the gang, evaded capture by the Italian police as they criss-crossed the crowded, and gridlocked, streets of the Italian city, before being driven up a ramp onto the deck of a Bedford VAL bus with Harrington bodywork for unloading. Although much of the chase sequence was filmed on location in Italy, one of the most memorable elements of the chase – that through the sewers – was in fact filmed in Coventry. The film was also notable as being the final appearance in film of the noted British writer, actor and director Sir Noël Coward; the uncle of the film's director, he was to retire after its making and died four years later.

■ **LEFT: Like the red, white and blue Minis used in *The Italian Job*.**

■ **BELOW: Mark Wahlberg and Charlize Theron arrive for the premiere of *The Italian Job*.**

THE ITALIAN JOB

There's no other car like a Mini. There's never been a Mini like the Italian Job.

Drive it. And find out how to have real fun. There's nothing to touch the Italian Job.

It's got the style you want. With all the fun you deserve. At a price that won't break the bank. The Italian Job. Stealing all the attention; with sporty looks and nippy performance. Dressed to thrill; with cool style, down to the very last detail. Ready to escape and go places; whether you're tackling the hairpins at Monte Carlo, or beating the rush around Hyde Park Corner. The Italian Job. Get behind the wheel; and get away with it.

■ **ABOVE: Rowan Atkinson in a Mini at Goodwood Circuit in 2009.**

■ **RIGHT: Mr Bean in his yellow Mini.**

This seminal British film is not, however, to be confused with the 2003 version directed by F. Gary Gray and starring Mark Wahlberg in the role of Charlie Croker made famous by Caine. With the action in the remake shifted to Los Angeles and Venice, the one common thread was the use of BMW-produced MINIs during the car chase.

Another British film to feature a Mini prominently is *Mr Bean's Holiday*, which starred the comedian Rowan Atkinson in the accident-prone title role. Directed by Steve Bendelack and released in 2007, the film portrayed the hapless Mr Bean on a journey across France for a holiday on the French Riviera. The car used for the film carried the registration YGL 572T; a second Mini, (this time a left-hand drive version is also seen in the film), is driven with a French registration by the character Sabine. This was the second film to feature the character Mr Bean; the original movie – *Mr Bean* of 1997 that was directed by fellow comedian Mel Smith – originally included a sequence of a Mini being driven round Harrods although this failed to make the film's final edit.

The film was a spin-off from a television series – *Mr Bean* – that ran originally for five years from 1990 until 1995, although it has been regularly repeated since then. The first car to appear in the television series was a Mini Mark II dating originally from 1969. Registered RNT 996H, this car was destroyed in an off-screen accident at the end of the first episode. This vehicle was replaced in subsequent episodes by a later, 1976, example – SLW 287R. There were a number of running gags featuring the car during the course of the series, particularly involving the car's security. In the episode of the series entitled *Back to School*, *Mr Bean*, one of the Minis featured was crushed by a tank. Following the demise of the live-action series, there was an animated version running for 26 episodes made in 2002; this too featured a Mini.

Another classic television series to make use of a Mini-derived vehicle was the cult series *The Prisoner*. Filmed in Portmeirion and starring Patrick McGoohan, the series ran to 17 episodes broadcast originally in 1967 and 1968. A Mini Moke was to feature

prominently in the series.

A second British television series of the 1960s, *Randall and Hopkirk (Deceased)*, featured a red Mini – registration number BAP 245B – which was originally driven by Marty Hopkirk (played by Kenneth Cope), who was killed in the first episode and was subsequently driven by Hopkirk's widow Jeannie (played by the Australian actress Annette Andre). The television series, which was produced by ITC Entertainment for ITV, was to run for 26 episodes. The whole run was filmed in 1968 and 1969 and shown in 1969 and 1970. In 2000 the series was remade starring the comedians Bob Mortimer and Vic Reeves, though the remake didn't include the original Mini. Although believed still to be extant, the car used in the making of the series

■ BELOW: **Patrick McGoohan appears to be looking at his exact double in *The Schizoid Man* episode of the CBS television series *The Prisoner*.**

has disappeared from the records.

In 1984 a BBC television series called *Driving Ambition* was made starring Rosemary Martin as Donna Hewitt a housewife who, in conjunction with her local garage mechanic (a role played by Gavin Richards), converts her Mini into a sports car in order to take on the male-dominated world of motor sport. Ultimately, and inevitably, she proved triumphant as the Mini defeated a Vauxhall Firenza at Brands Hatch.

■ **ABOVE INSET: Annette Andre plays Jeannie in *Randall and Hopkirk (Deceased)*.**

It was not only in Britain that the Mini made its mark in film. There was also a film from New Zealand, directed by Geoff Murphy and released in 1981, called *Goodbye Pork Pie* in which a hired yellow Mini – nicknamed Pork Pie – travels the country whilst the local police try to stop the couple in the car – who become known as the Blondini Boys – from reaching their destination. Promoted with the strap line 'Calling all cars – Stop that yellow Mini!' the film's promotional material prominently featured a Mini being hotly pursued by the forces of law and order.

In 2002, the MINI Cooper appeared in the film *Austin Powers Goldmember*, which was directed by Jay Roach. In the film Mike Myers, in his guise as Austin Powers, travels back to 1975 after learning that his father had been kidnapped by an associate of Dr Evil called Goldmember. A total of six red cars were supplied to the film's producers for transformation into Austin Powers spy cars.

In 2007 a MINI Cooper Convertible was to be used in the comedy

Heartbreak Kid. Directed by Bobby and Peter Farrelly, the film revolves around a recently married man, played by Ben Stiller, who, although believing himself to have married the perfect woman, meets another woman on his honeymoon. The car is used regularly during the film as the location for animated discussions between the married couple.

Other notable film and television appearances include appearing as a psychedelic version in the Beatles' film *Magical Mystery Tour* (1967), as a classic car in *Lara Croft: Tomb Raider* (2001) and in a car chase in *The Bourne Identity* (2002). Peter Sellers' bespoke Mini – it had wicker side-panels provided by Hooper – was to feature in one of the classic Inspector Clouseau films – the late Blake Edwards-directed *A Shot in the Dark* – of 1964.

Although Sir Alec Issigonis was quoted as saying, in *Crash: The Limits of Car Safety* by Nicholas Faith and published in 1997, that 'I make all my cars with such good brakes, such good steering, that if people get into a crash it's their own fault,' the fact that there were crashes is undeniable.

■ ABOVE INSET: **The mangled wreckage in which pop star, Marc Bolan, lost his life.**

On 16 September 1977 the musician Marc Bolan, of the group T. Rex, was killed when he was a passenger in a purple Mini 1275GT (registration FOX 661L) being driven by his girlfriend, the American musician Gloria Jones. The car hit a sycamore tree in Barnes, southwest London. Over the years, a memorial to the musician has grown up at the accident spot and in 2007 the site was officially recognised as Bolan's Rock Shrine.

As in the 1960s, the new MINI has become a car of choice for many involved in sport and culture. Amongst noted celebrity owners are or have been the following actors – Rowan Atkinson, Whoopi Goldberg and Elijah Wood – the following musicians – Noel Gallagher, Elton John, Madonna, Sting and Robbie Williams plus the impresario Simon Cowell – and footballers such as the late George Best and Ryan Giggs. Other notable owners include the creator of the Harry Potter novels, J. K. Rowling, the Formula One driver, Juan Pablo Montoya, the magician, Penn Jillette, and the highly successful rally driver from the 1960s, Paddy Hopkirk.

Customisation and Variants

Over the years, few models have had as long a life and been produced in so many variants – both official and unofficial – as the Mini and MINI. Amongst the variants offered on the original Mini were the following:

Wolseley Hornet and Riley Elf – produced between 1961 and 1969, with total production reaching 28,455 and 30,912, these were designed to be upmarket versions of the original Mini. The models were provided with larger boots that protruded from the rear and thus gave the car a more traditional look. The front end of the model was also modified to incorporate each marque's traditional grille. Both variants were also more lavishly appointed internally with, for example, a wood veneer dashboard. Originally they were fitted with the 848cc engine used in the more basic model but this was upgraded in 1963 to the 998cc engine used by the Mark II Cooper. Both models were also to be upgraded following the launch of the Mark III in 1966.

Morris Mini Traveller and Austin Mini Countryman – again launched in 1961 and with production also running through to 1969, these were two-door estate models of the car with production totalling 99,000 and 108,000 respectively. The vehicles were fitted with a chassis that was almost four inches longer than the original and the estate section was fitted with wooden inserts; these were non-structural but echoed the design of the earlier Morris Minor estate.

■ **RIGHT: A Mini Countryman brochure.**

■ **BELOW: The 1965 Riley Elf and Wolseley Hornet.**

■ **ABOVE: A 1961 Mini Van.**

■ **RIGHT: A 1976 Mini Pick-up 850.**

Mini Van – based around the chassis of the longer Mini Traveller, production of the Mini Van continued up until 1982 by which date more than 520,000 of the model had been constructed. Designed to have a capacity of about a quarter of a ton, the vehicle lacked rear side windows and, as it was classed as a commercial vehicle and therefore not liable for Purchase Tax, it proved highly popular until the imposition of the universal Value Added Tax. The vehicle was rebranded as the Mini 95 in 1978; the new name, which never really took off in Britain, was a reflection of its gross weight – 0.95 ton.

Mini Pick-up – constructed between 1961 and 1982, by which date just over 58,000 had been built, the Pick-up was based around the Mini Van although fitted with an open rear cargo platform and a tailgate. A basic model, the vehicle lacked a chrome grille and even a heater was not provided on the standard model.

Mini Moke – designed originally for the British Army as a lightweight vehicle similar to the US Jeep, the Moke – the name is derived from an

MINI VAN & PICK-UP

SUPERCOVER

Because the best cars deserve the best back-up

Applicable only to vehicles used within the United Kingdom

Supercover applies to every new vehicle detailed in this brochure. All you have to do is complete the supplied Registration card and post it to reach us within 30 days. It's one of the most comprehensive service schemes ever offered in the United Kingdom by any motor vehicle manufacturer.

At each stage in their production, vehicles are thoroughly examined by our experts and engineers. In addition, the dealer puts each vehicle through a long and extensive check.

So when you buy your new vehicle you can be confident that everything possible has been done to ensure that it is in perfect condition.

Supercover is a very comprehensive package. But if you have any trouble whatsoever, no matter how small, you just contact your dealer. He'll do his best to keep your vehicle in excellent condition.

If you're not 100% satisfied with the service you get, then we provide a special card with every vehicle, which should be sent direct to us so that we can make sure the problem is resolved quickly and efficiently.

Supercover is a permanent charter for the British motorist. It gives you one more reason for buying from the Austin Morris range.

Mini

from Austin Morris with Supercover.

Grosvenor House, Redditch, Worcestershire B97 4DQ

A pleasure to work with

If there is a more versatile vehicle than the Mini Van it can only be the Mini Pick-up with its spacious 26 ¾ cu. ft (0.76 m^3) capacity able to provide the answer to the transport problems of so many businesses (both large and small) throughout the country.

The simple fold-down tailgate gives easy access to the ample loadspace which is (like the Mini Van) a workable 1 ft 5 ½ in (0.44 m) from the ground. Also, the loadspace can be easily reached over the sides of the Pick-up which are only 2 ft 10 ¾ in (0.88 m) high.

The many advantages that apply to the Mini Van also apply to the Mini Pick-up. The small but powerful engine can handle both heavy work loads and town traffic conditions with equal ease, and when hard at work behind the wheel you can't fail to notice the excellent suspension and the effortless way with which the vehicle responds to your demands.

When you consider running costs, ease of maintenance and overall performance, the Mini Pick-up is sure to be the one for you.

Up in town, down on the farm or anywhere it's needed, the Mini Pick-up makes your work that much easier.

archaic English word for donkey – was manufactured between 1964 and 1993 at factories in Britain and overseas. Originally built at the Cowley factory in 1964, production shifted to Longbridge and, by the time domestic production ceased in 1968, some 14,500 had been built in the UK. Production in Australia commenced in 1966 with some 26,000 being constructed between then and 1981. A further 10,000 were built in Portugal between 1980 and 1993, when worldwide production of the Moke ceased. Although designed for military use, the model's low ground clearance and small wheels made it impractical as an off-road vehicle. It was, however, to find success as a beach buggy on

■ **ABOVE: The 1964 Mini Moke.**

■ **BELOW: An Australian Mini K.**

various Caribbean islands and in the Far East. Three examples were also to be found on Pitcairn Island – the only road vehicles to operate on this remote British territory in the Pacific and selected because they were light enough to be lifted by the island's only crane from the supply ship (there being no airport or dock serving the island).

Morris Mini K – produced exclusively for the Australian market – the 'K' stood for Kangaroo – this model was manufactured at BMC's factory at Zetland, New South Wales, for 30 months from early 1969 to August 1969. It was fitted with a 1098cc engine.

From the early 1980s onwards, recognising the potential from a marketing standpoint of the production of limited edition cars, the Mini was to appear in a whole range of such editions. These included the anniversary models such as the Mini 25 (5,000 produced in 1984 to mark the car's 25th anniversary), the Mini 30 (3,000 in 1989 to mark the 30th anniversary), the Mini 35 (1,000 in 1994) and the 40 (250 based around the Mini Cooper in 1999). There was also the London collection that included the Mini Ritz (3,725 in 1985), the Mini Piccadilly (2,500 in 1986) and the Mini Park Lane (4,000 in 1987). Other limited editions included the Mini Jet Black (3,000 in 1988), the Mini Sky (500 in 1989), the Mini Cooper Monte Carlo (200 in 1994), the Mini Paul Smith (1,800 in 1998; the designer also produced a one-off with 86 coloured stripes), the Mini Cooper Sports LE (100 in 1998) and the Mini John Cooper (300 in 1999). These models were produced both for the domestic and export market; there were also a number of limited edition models specifically for the export trade.

■ **BELOW: The Mini 40.**

These included the Mini After Eight for the French market (1,500 constructed in 1991) and the Mini Silver Bullet for Germany (400 produced in 1996).

All of the above models were manufactured by or on behalf of BMC and its successors; the Mini, however, has found its way into a vast array of kit cars and specials both in the United Kingdom and overseas. Amongst the models available were the Robert Mandry-designed Mini Scamp, the Deep Sanderson 301, which competed at Le Mans, the William Towns-designed Microdot City Car project, the Domino Pickup, the Midas, which is a development of the Mini Marcos that is available either as a kit or fully

■ ABOVE: The Mini 35.

■ LEFT: The Mini Ritz.

■ **ABOVE: The MINI Paul Smith.**

assembled, the Hustler T4, the Ogle SX1000 and the Unipower. There was even in the 1960s a motorhome version of the Mini – the Mini Wildgoose – that was based on the Mini Van. The conversion kit – which cost between £445 and £601 – enabled the rear section to be rebuilt and thus to accommodate a dining area with four seats and a double bed.

Since 2000, BMW have produced a range of concept cars that have

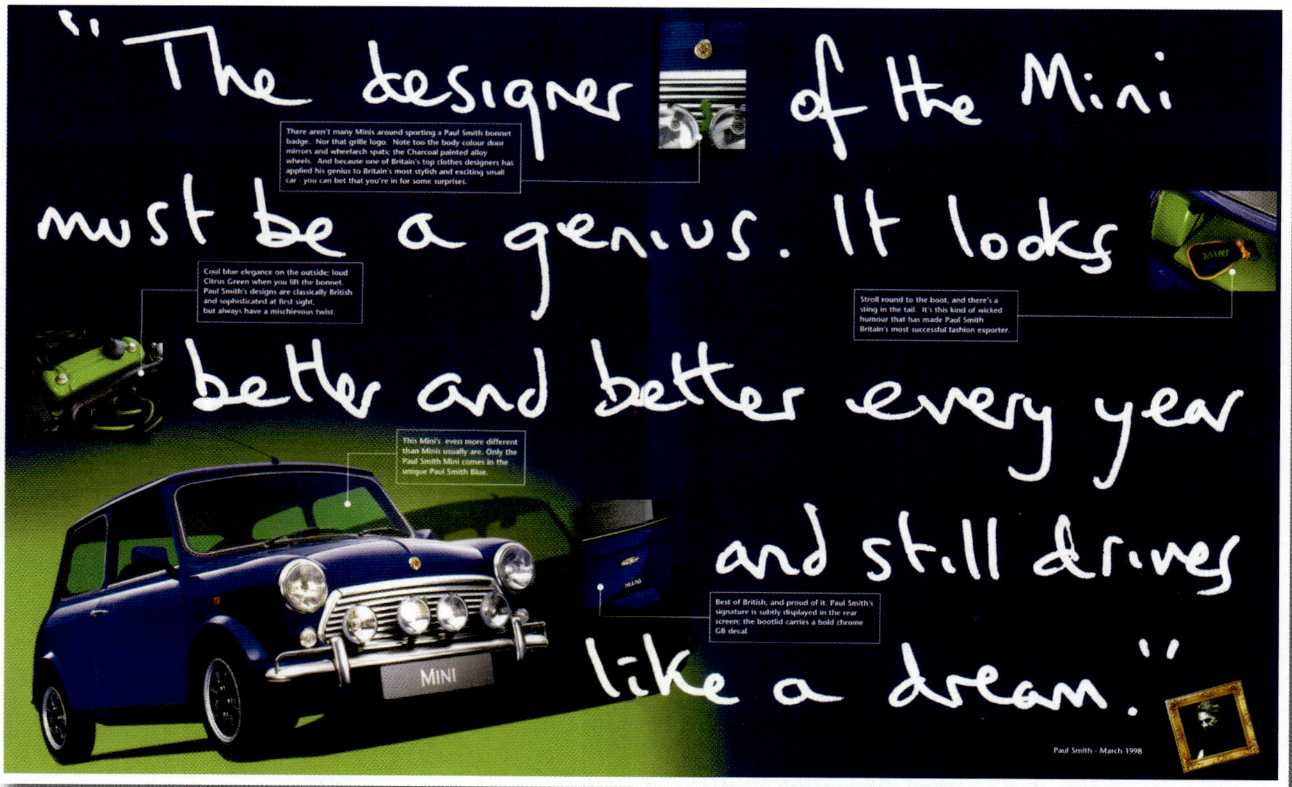

acted as prototypes for the further development of the MINI brand. These have included the MINI Traveller launched at the Frankfurt Motor Show in 2005. This was effectively an updated version, using the modern MINI as a base, of the classic Mini estate car. A second version, with modifications, was shown at the subsequent motor show in Tokyo. The eventual model emerged as the MINI Clubman in 2008.

Launched at the Paris Motor Show in 2008, the MINI Crossover was a four-metre long four-wheel vehicle; this was to enter production in 2010 as the MINI Countryman. The Countryman is the first modern MINI assembled outside the UK, with the work being undertaken by Magna Steyr in Austria. Unveiled at the Frankfurt Motor Show in 2009, the MINI Coupé was a two-seat vehicle. Fitted with a coupé body, the chrome radiator grille from the Cooper S and the engine from the John Cooper Works model, this car has yet to enter production, although it's likely to do so in 2011. Launched at the Detroit Motor Show in January 2010 was the MINI Beachcomber; based around the concept of the Mini Moke but heavily updated, the Beachcomber utilised the four-wheel chassis developed for the Countryman project. In order to protect its occupants from wind and rain the concept car features a soft-top roof. This protection can be completely removed from the body and stored in a container. There is also the possibility of using hardtop panels made of an extra-light plastic material, which protect the roof, the sides of the car and the rear storage compartment.

Two new concept cars were unveiled in early 2011. The first of these, launched at the January 2011 Detroit Motor Show, is the MINI Paceman. This three-door model again utilises the platform created for the Countryman but is fitted with a coupé body. The car, which is expected to enter production in 2012, is referred to as the MINI's first Sports Activity Coupé. A month later, at the Geneva Motor Show, the MINI Rocketman was unveiled. A foot shorter than the existing MINI and fitted

■ **ABOVE: The MINI Beachcomber concept car at the 2010 Geneva Motor Show.**
■ **BELOW: The MINI Traveller Tokyo concept.**

■ ABOVE AND RIGHT: **The MINI Coupé.**

with a three-door body, the car boasts a glass roof etched with a Union Flag – redolent of the classic Mini of the late 1960s – and is claimed to be able to achieve 94mpg.

So far all these models have been either petrol or diesel-powered. With the ever-increasing price of oil and growing concern about the level of greenhouse gases, MINI has also been exploring the use of alternative power for future vehicles. A concept

■ RIGHT: **The MINI Crossover concept.**

■ **ABOVE: The BMW MINI 4WD Countryman.**

■ **RIGHT AND INSET: The MINI Paceman concept.**

MINI with a hydrogen-powered internal combustion engine was unveiled at the 2001 Frankfurt Motor Show but much more significant is the development of the electrically-powered MINI – the MINI E. This was launched at the Los Angeles Motor Show in 2008. The choice of this fair was significant in that the State of California had introduced legislation requiring car manufacturers to offer vehicles with zero emissions. As part of the unveiling, BMW announced an initiative whereby up to 500 electrically-powered MINIs were to be available to lease to drivers in Los Angeles and the city of New York. The price of $850 per month didn't deter 10,000 from registering their interest in being involved in the 12-month pilot programme from June 2009; in May 2010 it was announced that the leases could be renewed for a further 12 months at $600 per month. A second trial was undertaken in the UK from December 2009 involving 40 cars. The British cars were leased at £330 per month. One car was also supplied to the British government for testing in official use. A trial in Germany using 100 cars began in September 2010 and a further trial area, this time China, started in February 2011.

The MINI E is largely manufactured

■ **ABOVE AND INSET: The MINI Rocketman concept car and interior.**

at Cowley but is shipped to Munich where the electrical equipment is fitted. Power is obtained from a lithium-iron battery pack which offers a theoretical maximum range of 156 miles – although much less than this in practice – and a top speed of 95mph. The electric motor is located under the bonnet where, historically, the internal combustion engine was located. As an electrically-powered vehicle, the MINI E is fitted with regenerative brakes; these are designed to capture the kinetic energy produced as the vehicle decelerates. Although designed for a maximum speed of 95mph, testing of one of the MINI Es around the Nurburgring showed that the car was capable of reaching 116mph, only 3mph less

■ ABOVE AND INSET: **The MINI E being charged and under the bonnet.**

than the fastest of the production versions of the existing car.

The trial of the MINI E proved there were a number of potential problems. The first of these was that the infrastructure was not yet in place for recharging the batteries as the number of garages with power-charging points was limited. A second problem concerned the size of the battery pack. The size required to ensure a reasonable range was such to require the removal of the rear passenger seats. A third issue was that, in particularly cold weather, the range of the battery was considerably reduced from the maximum level.

The official MINI E isn't the only version of an electric MINI on offer; Hybrid Technologies of Nevada, in the USA, have produced a version of the MINI Cooper using an all-lithium battery. Although the top speed of the model is lower than that of the MINI E, the vehicle does have a slightly greater practical range.

With developments such as the MINI E, the model is looking to the next generation of cars and, with its popularity around the world increasing, the model looks certain to have a long and prosperous future.

Afterword

It is no more than 50 years since the original Mini was launched and more than a decade since the arrival of the newer version. Both models first appeared at times of change; in the case of the former it was the period when Britain was gradually withdrawing from Empire and was a country increasingly marginalised in Europe and, in the case of the latter, it was to become a product fostered by a new owner as the once-mighty British Leyland entered a terminal decline. Both, however, established themselves as hugely successful and innovative models achieving great popularity at home and overseas. The original Mini is now recognised as one of the British design icons of the 20th century; the new MINI looks destined to achieve a similar status in the 21st.

Further information:

Books:

A Mini Adventure: 50 Years of the Iconic Small Car;
Martin Wainwright; Aurum Press; 2009

Maximum Mini: The Essential Book of Cars Based on the Original Mini;
Jeroen Booij; Veloce; 2009

Mini Restoration Manual;
Lindsay Porter; Haynes; 1998

Mini: A Celebration of Britain's Best-Loved Small Car;
Graham Robson; Haynes; 2006

Mini: An Intimate Biography;
Christy Campbell; Virgin Books; 2009

Mini: The Definitive History;
Jon Presnell; Haynes; 2009

Mini: The True and Secret History of the Making of a Motor Car;
Simon Garfield; Faber & Faber; 2009/2010

The Essential Buyer's Guide: Mini;
Mark Paxton; Veloce; 2009

The Mini;
Jon Presnell; Shire Library; 2010 (originally published 1994)

The Mini: Celebrating 50 Years of a Modern Motoring Icon;
Jeremy Clarkson and Brian Laban; Carlton Books; 2009

Magazines:

Mini Magazine; Future Publishing; monthly
Mini World; Kelsey Publishing; monthly
Modern MINI; Kelsey Publishing; bi-monthly

Websites:

forum.minicooper.org
www.britishmini.club.co.uk
www.m4minis.com
www.mini.co.uk
www.minicooper.org
www.MINImotorsports.com
www.miniworld.co.uk
www.mini2.com
www.theminiforum.co.uk